FURLOUGH

The Civil War Diaries
of
Sarah Belle Bright
and
Charles Alexander Elder
of
Trenton, Tennessee

1861-1867

Andrew Hays

Compiled and Annotated by
Robert Dudley Hays

HERITAGE BOOKS
2008

HERITAGE BOOKS

AN IMPRINT OF HERITAGE BOOKS, INC.

Books, CDs, and more—Worldwide

For our listing of thousands of titles see our website
at
www.HeritageBooks.com

Published 2008 by
HERITAGE BOOKS, INC.
Publishing Division
100 Railroad Ave. #104
Westminster, Maryland 21157

International Standard Book Numbers
Paperbound: 978-0-7884-4778-5
Clothbound: 978-0-7884-7479-8

Contents

Preface

The following is a transcription of the original diaries kept by my great-great-grandparents during the American Civil War. What began as an effort to share Charles and Belle Elder's diaries with their descendants became a serious project to publish the heart and soul, which their writings so poignantly illustrate. It is a true narrative of courage, honor, self-sacrifice and kindness. It is my hope that in publishing these diaries, the reader can be inspired by two young people, who despite being caught in the middle of a brutal and tragic war, managed to find strength in their faith in God and each other.

Andrew Hays
Winchester, Virginia

Introduction

This is a true story. It happened during those unfortunate, historic days when this country, divided against itself, was fighting for its very existence. The War Between the States was on, bringing with it all the attendant economic, political, and military problems which only a civil war could bring.

But there were personal and intimate problems too. Fathers were being called from the fireside to defend the home and family; young men with dreams were having those dreams interrupted to do bloody battle with their fellow citizen, not knowing when or if they would ever be able to resume the dreams and make them come true; women, young and old were finding themselves, perhaps for the first time, alone and face to face with a world which knew no favorites in time of war, and there were the problems which young people like Belle Bright and Charles Elder faced, the solution to which could only be found in their own character, their own young strength, and their own sense of responsibility.

Belle Bright in 1861 was just a wisp of a girl, eighteen years of age, who should have been looking forward to courtship and marriage and a happy life in the midst of a fairyland which was called Dixie. She was the daughter of a minister-professor who was then the head of a girls' academy in Trenton, Tennessee. Her grandfather was a Princeton professor, and had actually held the reins of that stately institution as its Acting President. Belle herself, although only eighteen, was a teacher in her father's academy.

Charles A. Elder was one of those thousands of young southern gentlemen who had been building dreams and making great plans for the future, but who instead had to leave friends and fireside to saddle a cavalry horse in defense of a principle which seemed more important. He was just twenty-three, and he was in love with Belle Bright.

The story that follows is one of heartbreak, tragedy, loneliness, and a constant search for a furlough from these emotional disturbances. But for the most part, it is a story of a struggle by two young and intelligent people caught up in the throes of a war which was brutal and relentless, and which divided this country in such a manner as has never been dreamed of before or since.

This story is told in their own words, through the diaries which they kept in the days when the diary was their most trusted friend and their greatest consolation. The diaries have been passed down through the family and are today still well-preserved and highly cherished possessions.

Today's young men and women of similar ages will be amazed at the intellectual manner in which Belle Bright and Charles Elder expressed themselves, and will probably be surprised at the adult perspective with which they faced some rather serious problems. Perhaps it was the intellectual family background which gave Belle Bright this peculiar ability to express herself in such a fine manner at so early an age, and young Charles Elder had also been exposed all his life to a type of individual existence and individual responsibility which were familiar to the Old South, but which have been somewhat lost in today's era of mass education and modernistic living.

As Belle Bright begins her diary on May 12, 1861, her thoughts are in many ways similar to the thoughts of millions of other young girls since that time, as they have watched their loved ones don the uniform of their country and march forward to war. As she writes, Charles has already received his summons to duty, and already their plans for the future have been necessarily altered.

Robert Dudley Hays

Belle's Diary

May 12, 1861

I went to the courtroom early to assist the ladies in making uniforms for the Confederate volunteers. Charley came up after a while, and stood near me. I don't know how it is, but God has answered my prayers and my heart has ripened into a warm affection for him. His rare sensibility, his unvarying kindness and love, his purity of character. He took his seat near me, talked quietly about many things, and I felt the sweetest happiness in having him near me. I realized that he was soon to leave. Oh, America, who would have thought that it would ever have been appropriate for your children to arm against each other! But the South must rise to arms! Ye brave, the patriot sword unsheathed, march on, all hearts resolved on liberty or death! How is it possible for us, the spoiled children of liberty with peace and the most unheard of prosperity, to realize this awful calamity? Would that I could shield all who are dear to me from this scourge.

May 15, 1861

I do not think my heart has known such depression and yet anticipated happiness as now. The Confederate volunteers have left; God alone knows how long to be absent! Charley has gone, and I am awakened to the warmth of my affection for him. He wants me to marry him.

Gibson County Courthouse, 1841-1899; it was torn down in 1899 to make room for the present one. Site of the "courtroom" mentioned in Belle's diary entry of May 12, 1861.
Photograph courtesy of Mr. Frederick Culp.

May 16, 1861

Charley is to be back in two weeks. If I am to be married there must be some preparation. I can scarcely realize it. Charley's wife! This happiness seemed to me so far in the future.

May 18,1861

Today is so beautiful, everything so fresh and cool and green. The sky a pale limpid blue as if it had a thin gossamer veil across its bosom. It is on such days that the heart lives in a sad sweet memory. So like days in an old year that we seem to live in them again. Happy days—are we to know them no more—are they, the purest and the sweetest I ever lived, to be but a happy glamour to compensate for dark ones coming on.

May 20, 1861

Pa permitted the school to march down to the depot to see our regiment pass by to Union City. I was disappointed though, as there was no Charley. I was indulging myself with the half-formed anticipation that he might spend Wednesday evening with me, but instead there came a letter which Marcus brought a few minutes before dinner.

Sabbath May 26, 1861

Camilla my cousin, has just returned from the depot, giving us an animated account of troops passing from Jackson on their way to Union City. Our boys though, I guess, will remain at Fort Randolph—have not heard from Charley since I wrote last Thursday night.

Wednesday morning May 28, 1861

Yesterday I received a long letter from Charley by one of the privates from Fort Randolph, Mr. W. Ivy. One also he had written to Pa. Charley gave me permission in a little note to read his letter before handing it to Pa. I did so. Last night Jenny (my cousin) and Dr. Means called. After they left I went into Ma's room, asked Pa if he could make out Charley's letter. He said he had read it with difficulty. As before he advised that we should not marry now, and I have no doubt but what he is right. Charley appealed to Pa's own youth when in similar circumstances he had loved and married. Pa said his judgment had condemned it as being precipitate, that he married at least two years before he should, and then Ma remarked that it had been the cause of much of their pecuniary embarrassments. She said positively she would give her consent to it under no circumstances in the world. Pa said that he supposed my main motive in marrying now was to throw a shield around Charley from temptation, but so far as his observation has gone he had always noticed that when a man would not sustain his worthiness of character during an engagement, it was seldom, very seldom, he ever did so after marriage; that this now should be Charley's test of character; if he passed through the ordeal manly, courageous, energetic, that then there might be no objection.

May 29, 1861

Yesterday morning Charley came on furlough. In the evening, Gussie (my sister) and I started to the depot to see some troops go by. Jennie went with us from B. Elders. Shook hands with Charley in the freight room. He talked with me awhile at the depot, and at twilight walked home with me. After tea, he came down and sat 'till late. I read Pa's letter in answer to his. Charley seemed more disappointed than I thought of his being. I do not know though but what it may be for the best...if he will only be spared through this war, then our union will be happier. God will bless us if we are guided by a sense of duty; if we are willing to deny ourselves present happiness because it is right.

June 2, 1861

My good journal (shall I call this that), I intend now writing my testimony. Ah! How uncertain to us are future transactions! How totally differently situated from what I anticipated two months ago! Charles a soldier and I probably his wife tonight, God forgive me if I have decided wrong. God forgive me if I've blinded my eyes to true duty to follow inclination. I am marrying in opposition to Ma and Pa...a thing I thought I never could have done. I sat down to review my motives. May my Heavenly Father enable me to study them. First , I think, is my and Charley's desire, and then probably if not now, we may never marry. For Charles to return to Fort Randolph sad and depressed would render me unhappy and fearful on his account, fearful that he would not sustain himself in the good resolutions he has been lately practicing, fearful he would lose energy and perseverance in his service, fearful most of all that the good impressions which I thank God have been made upon his heart would be erased, and himself farther from a Christian than ever. As his wife, may God create in me an ever strengthening, abiding determination to use every right exertion in influencing him for good. God knows that in this I am sincere. Charley tells me that his judgment does not condemn him, that he has confidence that he will be able to support us both. Oh, my Heavenly Father, preserve him! Now, I wish to go down and talk with Ma and Pa, as a daughter, endeavor to obtain their kindness if not their full and willing consent.

June 3, 1861

Married…and such a marriage! God knows if I have done wrong. This indifference I think, is wrong and undeserving. There is one wish in my heart paramount to everything, and that is to leave home. Charley's gone…he remained with me last night 'till four in the morning. Not one came in to bid us God speed. Pa has not spoken a word since yesterday morning about it. He says Belle is very dear to him…strange manifestation!…then he advised me against it but said he gave his consent because I told him it was for my happiness. I feel the neglect painfully. Ma knows how I feel. But I must <u>not</u> forget the duties and obligations I owe to them as a daughter. They have been considerate of my happiness, and I owe much to them, but what is every benefit in the world without love accompanying it? One cannot feel the warmth of loving gratitude for favors thus bestowed. Dear Charley…what would be my world without him. I felt such happiness last night, mingled with the deepest regret.

June 25, 1861

Charley's gone. He left me with a kiss at the depot, Before that we sat on the steps of the brick house.

June 18, 1861

Tonight is Thursday and my nineteenth birthday.

August 21, 1861

Today I've been reading "Woman in Her Social and Domestic Character", by Mrs. John Landford. I thought of it tonight while in the parlor. I did much that was uneasy, inelegant and perhaps ungraceful, but I hope I will have frequent opportunities of entering into society until I've become fully accustomed to it and can with impunity act without stiffness and formality, or I should have said hypocrisy. Mrs. Landford says that the true source of elegance is taste; to be truly elegant one must have feeling, but I must not write anymore tonight. It is late and I'm sleepy.

August 27, 1861

Charley is gone to Missouri. How I have looked forward to this week, counting the days industriously, glad that my teaching made them slip by so quickly, and with last week came a letter from dear Charley saying they would be ordered into the interior almost immediately. Oh, God grant their safe return. When the war was first announced, I did not have the apprehension I do now. I was haunted with the fear that it was the battle of Armageddon that was to be fought, and the immediate consequences of deaths and wounds did not bring the uneasiness that did the thoughts of being ushered into Eternity unprepared. Charley is sad and gloomy, and has, I fear, a feeling that he will never return. My heart sickens at the thought. Dear, dear Charley, so kind, so noble, so self-sacrificing. He said nothing of sadness in writing home. I think he knew it would give us unhappiness. We heard from another letter that he was very gloomy. It made me feel sad, but I loved him more.

August 28, 1861

Would, would this war was over! [sic] Today we heard of a battle in Missouri in which our boys were engaged. (*Note: This was one of the first battles fought across the Mississippi River from Columbus, Kentucky.*) God in Heaven, spare my Charley! I've prayed to God to preserve him from death and serious injury. I wish to commit our boys into God's hands in sincere faith, and then they will be preserved. How long, how long before we are again blessed with peace?

October 14, 1861

Monday, in my old home in Gussey's room...My journal, I do not love you. You seem irregular, broken, neglected, and so you are, poor book. You see how it is with my two homes (the Brights and the Elders) and not a very satisfying title to either. I've been a complete bird of passage between them, and most always I wanted you; you were just where I couldn't get you and so I scribbled just where it was most convenient, and therefore have scraps of my mind scattered here and there...in Charley's quotation book, in my school account book, in stray leaves and some in an old copy book. I would like quite well to have them together. Now good, I don't mean good, but book if you were a right cleanly, faithfully-kept book I would, I believe, be firmer to the promises I make you. Tonight, I've been thinking quite seriously I should be in a better spirit of writing more to you. Now if I had talked to you confidentially of Charley and me and other things when we were first married, if I had told you of him and me, how we loved and behaved during his visits, how we wrote and thought and felt when separated, how I came to make my first hasty visit to him at Columbus, returned and had him the day after come to see me and spend some few days, how what a happy, happy time we had, scarcely a shadow, how he left me with a half anticipation of being sent for too soon to spend some time, how hope rose and subsided and at last almost despaired, how one evening after wishing and looking for a letter and was disappointed, how I went out calling with Ma and Pa, how I came back and after a while got out my Sabbath school books and went to work, poorly enough though to study my lesson and how Gussey came upstairs and told me Charley had telegraphed for me to come. Oh, what a joy, what a thrill! How happy I was packing my trunk and getting ready. How Father and I went to the depot and the train didn't come, and we went home again, how I took off my bonnet and knelt down with my clothes, furs, and wrappings on trying to be reconciled when I heard the cars, sprang up, tied on my bonnet, ran downstairs, made Father consent to go, ran back to the depot, and after a great many ridiculous accidents was almost lifted into the car by Father, walked through two long cars unattended and at last was helped to a seat by a gentleman, how I laughed at my ridiculous rush and debut into the train, how when I got to Union City who should come into the train but Charley himself, who having almost despaired of my coming was on his way home, how we arrived safely at Columbus about cold, damp dawn and, having no conveyance, walked from the depot to Dr. Jackson's where Charley had with great difficulty secured my board. Charley and I rode out to his encampment and saw and were greatly delighted at so many things; the beautiful scene from Columbus off the Mississippi River, the tents and great multitudes of soldiers, infantry and cavalry, how we walked up the hill with Captain Flemming's wife and Dr. Jackson, and saw Colonel Marks' regiment on dress drill. I do not write much now, my Journal. I do not read much, nor practice on the piano much. My employments which I used to so delight in have very seldom of late occupied me. I will wash my hair now and perhaps write more after a while. Time again. Gussey says it is a little after nine. My head feels quite elegant. I wish it would not get hard and harsh and bushy. Milla *(another sister)* is an original. I wonder what inward conception of mirth made her flash up from the table, seize something and commence beating on a tea kettle in the window to some boys who were beating a drum in the street. She did not say much, but I thought I heard her chuckle with ineffable delight as I passed quite near. She seems the very embodiment of life, mirth. She will, I expect, make an admirable woman when sobered by Christian principles. She has great intellect and, I think, much wit. She has just lain down with the expression, "When I get rich and grown, I'm going to have linen sheets on my bed." There's a train. Oh, these war times! How great will be the blessings of peace, our dear ones with us, peace and prosperity restored, citizens again engaged in peaceful pursuits…no excitement …no irregularity, no frightening rumors, but peace, quiet, going to bed without fear, hoping and trusting in God, quiet rising in the morning with a calm trusting spirit of the day. Oh, when will such a time return! Perhaps our separation now, Charley, is but to prepare us to appreciate and thank God for the blessing of being at last permitted to live together. God grant we may some day be thus blessed. Dear, dear Charley.

October 18, 1861

There's one of my resolutions I fear I break repeatedly and that is in trying to cultivate grace, ease and elegance of manner. I resolve today to make my vow literal, to at dinner help myself but once to everything, to eat but one piece of bread no matter if used for dessert, to eat and help myself just as I would were I at Mother's table. It seems very trite perhaps to be making resolutions about things about which others scarcely give a thought, but I find it almost necessary to govern myself and retain my self respect.

November 10, 1861

It is Sabbath afternoon in this the last month of Autumn. I've sat near this window often before writing...both in the Spring and during the Summer. The first month after I became a wife, the aspens out the window were in green leaf, the foliage was green, honeysuckle and sweet woodvine were in bloom. I remember the second day, I believe it was, after our marriage, of folding a branch of honeysuckle and a rich rosebud in an envelope and putting them away to look at some other time. Now the aspen branches are getting bare, brown leaves are stealing in among the green ones like gray hairs on an old man's head. Now the far off foliage has a black purplish lustre, and the trees nearer are crisp and bare looking. The wind is blowing today from the South. That seems like Spring, doesn't it good book? The sky is a misty blue, looking like a tender blue eye that may at any time become suffused in tears.

Way off towards the horizon it deepens into a faint purple and the white clouds dreamily skimming its surface seem less defined. The wind stops now and then, and then the sunlight steals over us. It is a sweet, subdued evening, except this occasional sighing of nature. Ah! But who knows Autumn without its sighs!

November 29, 1861

Good Journal, I must have a nice clean page to write what's in my heart. There's been a sunbeam in my life. There's been a silver-golden tinted cloud in my sky. There's been a wave of softest, gentlest undulation over my ocean. A zephyr of sweetest odor, a strain of witching melody. A bouquet of all Earth's beauties in my yesterday, my good book. I've had almost a day, sweetest, brightest day of almost unalloyed pleasure. I've been to Columbus, now hallowed by memory's sweetest smile. I've been to the Buchannan house, which has received a day of beauty. I've been to Dr. Hoke's, whose house has been bathed in illumination from the glad light of my heart. I've been with Charley! He was so loving and I, may I thank God humbly that He enabled me to better conduct myself as a wife. We rode out one day and Charley told me we would have our marriage life always bright, that we would not let the clouds come to mar it. How earnestly I hope we may, that perfect love and perfect confidence may ever dwell between us! That in tribulation we may be ever hopeful, humble and grateful to God, that in happiness we may ever be grateful for every blessing and ever mindful of Him, ever believing, ever faithful. How long has it been since first I became so deeply serious about religion, two years this Fall. Since then, what has been my experience? My mind is still oftentimes clouded. While I was reading tonight, I had a strange feeling, it seemed of deep delight, of real satisfaction. There seems to be such a wide field for thought. If my life is prolonged, surely some day, if I'm patient and industrious, my mind will be some time emancipated from its strange thralldom, and I will be enabled to look upon all things freely and with a mind enabled to reason clearly and be convinced of truth, to hold the truth in consciousness without these ever painful recurring feelings at the mere suggestions of unbelief, when I can with a enlightened intellect face them boldly, battle down each one of their apparent strongholds without being weakened whatever in my own strength.

December 2, 1861

Monday night, Old Home…Six months ago today I became a wife. How blessed have I been since, of how much happiness has it been the forerunner. I had little idea then of the incidents that have transpired since. My book, I have known almost another week of almost unalloyed happiness. Charley came up a week ago last Friday, and left last Friday at noon. We were very happy during the week. He was very kind, loving and gentle. Dear, dear Charley, few appreciate him as he should be. He is gone now I am again a teacher. Today has been cold and damp and snowy.

December 31, 1861

This morning after reading my Bible and saying my prayers I wrote to Charley. Pa carried it to the depot and delivered it to Mr. Willicot Jones. Charley has perhaps received it by now. I hope so. I hope he is happy, hope he loves me deeply, warmly.

After sending my letter, I practiced an hour on the piano, about half an hour at scales and exercise, and the rest in singing "My Father Land". I think this is its name. I swept Ma's room, the entry, the front and back porches, raised a window and then sat down in the rocking chair. I was alone. I felt for a while a strange happy feeling in my heart. It was so beautiful, so very beautiful. The scene around me. The open doors, the raised window, the sunshine stealing in so soft, so warm so silently, Margaret's (my cousin) low humming, the click of her iron, all had a strange spell that seemed to make my heart happy and peaceful. I thought of Ma's having a can of peaches not quite eaten up. I got it down, helped myself, poured milk over it and then cream. After supper I went to the cream mug and drank cream alone. I do not like the effect and perhaps will not drink any more and, another thing, I wish to break myself of eating between meals. You are greatly despoiled, poor book, you have been greatly maltreated and neglected. My next book I wish to get smaller and to keep neat and nice and faithfully throughout. The end of next year, if I live and am well, I hope will find my journal neatly and faithfully kept. I hope will find my resolutions all faithfully kept. Oh! Next New Year! Next New Year! Where will it find us? I pray it will find me a Christian, that it may find me a noble and a better woman. I pray God it may find Charley and me farther in our efforts and desires to live pure and holy lives. I pray it may find us firm and established in faith and in doctrine. Oh! May we never as we grow older, grow less desirous of doing right. May we never grow less in love. May our marriage life never be a disappointment to us through our own wrong-doing. May we never have to look back upon our thoughts and endeavors as but vain, romantic dreaming which reality has shown us to be false, but may we find them expanding, growing firmer in practice. Oh! Charley, may we be faithful to ourselves. May God make us faithful to Him. If unhappiness is ever ours, may we bear it together. With hearts warmly and strongly interwoven, may sorrow never reach us with sympathies separate. My love has grown for him in the last year, dearest Charley, were you here I think you would write "my love has grown for Belle." I pray God it may ever grow. Good book, good-bye.

Sabbath night, March 16, 1862

I am in Father's office. They say they have been hearing the cannon today, supposed to be from New Madrid. I do not know what to think of Charley. I suppose he is there. Oh! It is strange to realize this. Later...I have learned that Charley has left New Madrid and is now in Corinth. Oh, how deeply grateful we should be!

Note

Although Belle Bright was at this moment expressing her gratitude over the fact that Charley was apparently out of danger, actually he was being drawn into one of the most fiercely-fought and memorable battles of the entire war...the famous Battle of Shiloh. Scene of the first major engagement in the western campaigns of the War Between the States, Shiloh was a struggle between Northern and Southern armies composed largely of unseasoned troops. The dogged determination and tenacity shown by Union and Confederate soldiers alike upon this battlefield made it an inspiring memorial to American courage. Fought in heavily wooded terrain, upon rain-soaked ground, the battle was marked by great confusion that prevailed generally on both sides. At the end of the first day, a great victory seemed to be within the grasp of the South. Overnight, heavy reinforcements joined the Northern Army and, on the second day, the Union troops forced the Confederates to retire from the battlefield and to retreat southward. The battle opened the way for the Union forces to gain possession of the Mississippi River during the following year, and to split the Confederacy with the capture of Vicksburg.

After the capture of Fort Henry and Fort Donelson by the North in February 1862, the Confederates, commanded by General Albert Sidney Johnston, had withdrawn southward, abandoning all of Kentucky and most of Tennessee west of the mountains. They formed a new line of defense along the railroad which ran from Memphis, on the Mississippi River, to Chattanooga. Johnston concentrated about 44,000 men at the important rail center of Corinth, Mississippi. In the meantime, a Federal army of 40,000 men commanded by General Ulysses S. Grant, had moved up the Tennessee River to Pittsburg Landing, 22 miles from Corinth. It was Grant's plan to wait at Pittsburg Landing until General Buell's army from Nashville should join him. Then the two combined armies would attack the Confederates in Corinth.

When General Johnston learned that Buell's army would reinforce Grant in a few days, he determined to attack before Buell arrived. His plan was to drive a wedge between the Union Army and the river to force Grant away from the Northern Army's base of supplies at Pittsburg Landing. Johnston then planned to turn upon Buell.

After marching from Corinth over rain-drenched roads, the Confederates reached the vicinity of Shiloh on the late afternoon of April 5, 1862. The following morning, they struck the Federal camps along the south and west fronts shortly after daybreak. Charley Elder with his regiment, the 4th Tennessee Volunteers, was engaged in some of the most stubborn fighting of the day which occurred near Shiloh Church, a small log structure after which the battlefield is named, and which the Union right held tenaciously as it stood at the intersection of strategically important roads. It was about ten o'clock in the morning when the 4th Tennessee was thrown into action and led an attack against the Federal Forces in the vicinity of the church, who fell back before the Confederate assaults.

In the meantime, the Northern center and left center had fallen back to positions known as the Hornets' Nest and the Peach Orchard. Here the heaviest fighting of the day continued for hours. In the Hornets' Nest, a natural fortress of dense woods and thickets, the Union line held firmly, driving back one Confederate assault after another. While directing an attack against the Federal left near the Peach Orchard, General Johnston was struck in the leg by a rifle ball. He died from the loss of blood about 2:30 in the afternoon. Late in the afternoon the Confederates finally closed in upon Prentiss's Union division in the Hornets' Nest, and forced him to surrender, together with 2,200 men.

The Union Army continued to retreat and by the end of the day it had been driven from one to three miles. At sunset, the army stood on the bluffs above Pittsburg Landing with its back to the river. Here it rallied, however, and drove back the last Confederate attacks of the day.

During the night, about 25,000 fresh Union troops, largely from General Buell's army, arrived to reinforce Grant. On the morning of April 7, the Confederates with 34,000 men faced Union forces numbering 54,000. Greatly outnumbered, the Confederates were forced to give ground as the battle progressed. At two o'clock in the afternoon, the new Confederate commander, General P.G.T. Beauregard, ordered his army to withdraw from the battlefield, and it fell back to Corinth.

The losses for the North in the two days' battle in killed, wounded, and missing were 13,017; for the South, 10,699. There were about 100,000 men engaged in the two-day struggle, which took place in a small area about six miles wide, with a tragic casualty rate of about one out of every four men engaged. Lieutenant Charles Elder lost his company commander in this battle and the mantle of company command fell on his shoulders as the 4th Tennessee Volunteers enjoyed and suffered fluctuating fortunes. The official report of their Colonel (O.F. Strahl, regimental commander) said that their casualties in this battle of April 6 and 7, 1862, were 219 killed and wounded. Here are excerpts from Colonel Strahl's official report of the part played by this volunteer regiment:

The position occupied by this regiment on the morning of the 6th was on the right of the 2nd Brigade, First Army Corps, and moved forward in the second line of battle until about 10:00 A.M. when we came up with the first line, which had been driven back by a battery of the enemy, placed on the opposite side of an old field on a hill. Here we were thrown into some confusion by the line of battle falling back through ours (this regiment was thrown in as a reserve); but we soon rallied and formed in front under a very heavy fire of grape and shell from the enemy's guns, which were about 800 yards distant. Our men here were ordered to fall flat on their faces in order to protect themselves, and while remaining here, General Stewart rode up and told me that General Bragg said that the battery must be taken, and asked me if I would do it. I told him we would try, and immediately ordered the men forward, bearing to the left in order to avoid the open field in front, and marched through a thicket of small timber at double quick. We continued to march at double quick until we were within 30 paces of the enemy's guns, when we halted, fired one round, rushed forward and took the battery. During the whole of this charge, the battery played upon us with grape and canister, making sad havoc in our ranks, killing 31 men and wounding about 160. The battery, however, according to the report of the prisoners taken, was supported by seven regiments of infantry.

After taking the battery, I found I was in advance of our lines for near a quarter of a mile, and we were heavily pressed both on the right and left by the enemy infantry. I immediately dispatched my adjutant for aid and in a short time had the pleasure of seeing our troops coming at the double quick to support me.

While remaining here, we were called on to support one of our own batteries that had been placed on the same ground that the enemy's battery had formerly occupied. While supporting this battery, we were in a very heavy fire from the enemy, who made a desperate effort to take it. We had several men wounded here, but the enemy were repulsed. We continued in line until after dark, when we fell back in order to get out of the reach of the enemy's gun boats. We slept where we had taken the enemy's battery, in their camp, and took supper and breakfast at their expense.

Then, on the second fateful day as the tide of battle turned against the Southerners, Colonel Strahl continues his official report:

> On Monday morning we were placed near the left of our line of battle. We were compelled to fall to the rear. I rallied my men and led them forward several times, but they were compelled to fall back. I finally placed my men on the left of a battery of the Washington Artillery and supported it until our whole line had fallen back on the hill on our rear. We then fell back just in time to save our men from our own guns, which opened with three shells in the direction of the position we had just left. The company and officers acted gallantly and fearlessly during both days of the fight, and rather appeared to court death than to fear it. My men acted gallantly the whole time, enduring the fatigue and danger without murmur.

And then in the following month Belle Bright confides in her diary:

May 13, 1862

Almost a month since I have written. You are a poor neglected friend, and I suppose I may congratulate myself that you are a book. I might not talk to you in this way were you a person, for then you would grow haughty and thus prevent my return. But instead, poor humble, mute friend, you lie still and neglected in my trunk, no complaint, no reproach when I take you up in my hands and then perhaps lay you aside without opening you, but I still feel better that I have you, and now poor book, I have come at last. I am a married woman now, you know, and there's somebody else to fill up my little moments which otherwise I might spend with you. I have been growing in heart and in life since when I first commenced neglecting you. It is not because I have not thought and felt deeply, and such thoughts and feeling which I would have perhaps enjoyed writing, but the time has flitted. The days and the moments have sung out their notes in my soul's bell. Some were hopeful, some were sad, some were but a low, gloomy tolling, but I did not write them, and if my soul still holds the graves of their bodies, or if they have but floated away forgotten and traceless, I do not know. Circumstances around me have been so different from my girlhood. Were they ushered by a High o'er ruling Hand, good book? Was some unseen Power guiding me? Is it with me still? Woman's is a strange destiny!

May 20, 1862

Charley is with me today. I dearly love his boyish manners and hope he will ever retain them.

June 20, 1862

Two weeks ago, Charley left home for safety from the Federals, whom we have heard were at Jackson. The rumor proved to be false and he returned the same evening. On Sunday the rumor was confirmed, but Charley concluded to remain overnight. We took tea with Mother and then went to Church. Next morning, Charley left for their hiding place. Wednesday, Cousin William drove me into town and I saw the Federals scattered about in different directions. The next morning, I went to the back gate to wait for Charley. Before getting to the gate, I saw him. I was so happy. It is so happy to love and trust that you are loved. He left again this morning. If I hear nothing to the contrary, I shall look for him again Sabbath night. I must be happy and pray and put trust in God.

June 23, 1862

My little book, a good little friend, my embodiment, patience and silent sympathy, harken while I place a bit of confidence in you. Charley was with me last night. He came late on horseback. I was very glad to see him. He says they have not been so much troubled by the soldiers for the last two, three days. He thinks it will be better for the refugee soldiers to return quietly to town. I think they would risk something. Saturday evening, a sudden notion came into my head to have Cousin Eliza cut my hair. My hair felt as if it needed washing and so I concluded from various impulses, I believe you may call them, to have my hair cut. Cousin got the big shears and shingled it short and close. So, my little book, you can imagine what an ugly somebody is writing to you! It will be some time, I guess, before it is long enough to look curly and not so stiff and bobbed. This I should all quietly take as a punishment to my foolishness. It is strange why I am thus hurried into acts which experience has taught me I nearly always regret.

July 16, 1862, Wednesday Morning

I am not so faithful as I would like to be in writing. Charley is gone, left on the 14th, Monday night. A long, long time has he been with me. Many sweet moments have we spent together, moments that in after years will come welling up in our memories as sweet melodies. Oh! how dear they were, how dear they are now! They've gone, little book but we must not be sad. Perhaps in the near future they will come again. May God teach us to improve them with a better heart, to enjoy with more gratitude and more love to Him. Cousin William drove me out Tuesday, 24th of June, to Mr. Davidson's to meet Charley. We had a happy time there. The house was quiet and orderly and cleanly kept. Mr. and Mrs. Davidson were from Middle Tennessee. Our long walks in the woods gathering blackberries, my hand in his. Charley one day fed "Shep" as he called me after my hair was so closely cut, but came to the conclusion that it would take a great many blackberries to fill my mouth. We left Saturday, 5th of July. We have been so happy together of late. I could not write down all of Charley's tenderness and care. It is very dear to be loved so. It is a great blessing to possess so warm and loving a heart. He has gone now, gone back to the army, to search his way carefully through the enemy's forces intervening. It is duty, though, and I am much happier in this than if he had remained with me in violation of it. Now I can pray for God's blessing, and hope for it.

July 20, 1862

'Tis Sabbath morning…just such a morning as I love through Summer. It has been raining, delightfully cool in large drops, sparkling mid the glazed aspen leaves and cedar sprays. I enjoyed it. Dear, dear Charley, how long is this separation to last? Oh, would your own heart may be sustained, strengthened, through trust in God. It may be years before this struggle is over…years before we are permitted to sit down under our own vine and fig trees at peace. God in Heaven spare him to me. God grant he may survive this war. Will our hearts be strengthened and made better. Will we be made a truer man and woman. To such ends these troubled times may be attuned. It is in our power through God's grace to make them our great blessing.

July 29, 1862

This is a warm day and I am not well. No, I feel badly...for almost four weeks I've been mostly this way. I wish I had someone to advise me in regard to the course to pursue with myself, if I am indeed affected as some have intimated to me. It is not right that I should be so ignorant. How wrong to let this branch of instruction be omitted in female education; what scarcely more important! I wish I could learn. If I ever become the Mother of a family, I shall instruct my daughter in regard to it. There's a load on my chest that renders breathing difficult...should I eat or not?...I can do with hunger, but I believe I've felt better when eating my regular meals.

January 25, 1863

Little book, it has been some time since I've written. It is not negligence though, but I concluded to omit writing, reading, and music until I had prepared sufficiently for my confinement. Do I endeavor as I should to be a Christian? God aid me. God aid Charley, too. Where is my husband today?

May 7, 1863

My little boy baby is in his crib. My husband-soldier is at home, sitting before the fire reading the history of Greece. I have both to live for!

Charley's Diary

Even though Belle Bright had already suffered through the many miseries of loneliness, separation, and all of the other attending heartaches of a nation at war with itself, there still remained for her a tragedy which would test all of her strength of character and her invincible faith in God upon which she had relied so often. How she made her way through the dark days of this tragedy is not known, because the May 7, 1863 entry was the last one for a long, long time.

However, just a few weeks later, Charles Elder entered for the first time, an item in his own diary, a journal which not only told of the tragic news, but went on through part of the year 1864 with other tales of bitter war, bloodshed, execution, loneliness, separation, and fortunately, some measure of happiness.

The then Captain Elder writes:

June 5, 1863 Friday Evening

This evening, somber in spirit as the cloud which hides the Heavens, I come to write. I come to record the first real great sorrow of my young life. Day before yesterday…3rd of June…my little child died. He was born in Trenton, Tennessee, which was then a Federal camp. I was a soldier for the South and was not there at his birth. He lacked one day of being two weeks old when I saw him. When Trenton was evacuated by the Union soldiers, I returned to my home, and since that time I never ceased to watch over the little child, even for a day. My Belle did not think he was going to die. She nursed him in her own arms much of the day. She watched over him in silence; in anguish; in tears; yes, in hope, too, and it was well, for it kept her bleeding heart from sinking. Oh, God thy mercy be on us!

Note

It is in early February of 1864 before any further records are seen in Captain Elder's journal. The third winter of the War finds the South fighting with its back more and more to the wall. Their victories are more infrequent and although a battle may be won, the pattern of conflict is one of continual retreat.

As Captain Elder resumes his diary he is being attached to General Humes's staff. From then on, that is for this last discouraging year of the war, he was the acting adjutant and aide de camp of General Humes, who was a brigade commander in Wheeler's cavalry, a force of some four thousand horsemen, which was protecting the continued retreat of the Confederate Armies as they fell back from Chattanooga, fought to defend Atlanta, and then as they retreated in the last days of the war from Savannah and Charleston, and made their final stand near Columbia, South Carolina.

And so, while Belle Bright prayed for the safety and waited hopefully for the eventual return of her beloved husband, Captain Elder was in the midst of some of the most dangerous activity of the entire war. However, as his diary and journal picks up in early 1864, his principle concern seems not to be of himself and the great danger of war, but rather for his beloved Belle, his fellow comrades, and his country, which is being torn apart in such a brutal manner.

February 7, 1864 Rome, Georgia

"That life is long and that answers life's great end." Well, little book! I commence to record my life in you with the commencement of my life in this state. I'm vexed that this paper of which you are made is so worthless. On your stained pages I continue my chronicle of the war. This is Sunday evening. On the night of the 3rd I arrived in Dalton—famous Dalton. A place where the eyes and interests of two nations are resting; on whose hills are resting and waiting in sullen silence the soldiers who are the hope and security of poor, suffering Southland. Here and reposing around Dalton are the men whom our enemies fear and hate. Around Dalton lie the shattered remains of our proud, heroic army which has struggled through blood to a score of victories and fled in shame from one inglorious defeat. Horrors of Shiloh!

In little, dreary, war-scarred Dalton, I arrived on Wednesday night and paid $5.00 to sleep from eleven until daylight in a dirty bed in an ugly garret hole. Next morning early I got "Orion" off the train—gaunt, frightened and looking as though he had nothing to eat for two weeks. I then reported to General Wheeler to find my future headquarters and be assured 'little confidant' that surprise and vexation mingled in my mind when I was ordered to report to General Humes at Oxford, Alabama, away in the interior about 120 miles. I had traveled from Panola, Mississippi to Dalton, Georgia, and been enroute for more than two weeks, all the way vexed, buffeted, mad. Had been detained in Grenada two or three days; in Jackson, Mississippi two days; in Meridian three days; in Montgomery three days; in Atlanta 20 hours; and then to get to Dalton sorely tired and worn and find that four days ride lay still before me over mountainous ways. All around me loomed in barren greatness the chain of hills frowning in the distance like threatening low clouds. My way seemed hemmed in with mountains. I looked about me. Only before me there was no mountain. I would look behind soon and high and dark lay the mountain as though I had crossed it. On the way I thought of the land of my devotion, the home of my homage, the wife of earthly worship. Oh, loved ones of this great land. God in His Mercy and Power guard you! I thought much in these miles of going home. For the first time in a long while the way is clear. Darling Belle, I have a furlough, but my papers are wrong and I must see General Humes. Wonder what he will do with me? Wonder how he will appear? I thought him then a noble gentleman and a friend of mine. Wonder if he is indeed. Fearful times have made fearful developments. Hope and think though, I will find the General what he was as lieutenant and captain, I know. At General Wheeler's headquarters I was introduced to a little man, rather stooped, large head, black hair and whiskers, beautiful teeth, dressed in genteel large cavalry boots, gray private's jacket, low felt hat—and this was General Wheeler. He was very polished in manner and quite polite. Immediately entered into conversation with me as though I was distinguished.

Everywhere I meet old acquaintances. I met Elijah Bright and Lady in Meridian and they were very kind. I was much pleased with the grace and accomplishment of Mrs. Bright. Belle, they are anxious for me to bring you to stay with them during the war. Will you do it? Dearest, for nearly two months I have not heard from you. How long will it be ere I hear from you—ere I meet you? God grant soon.

February 8, 1864

This morning I left Rome, Georgia and traveled without incident to this little community. The country is rocky and mountainous. Tonight I am with an old friend and acquaintance of Major Huestin and Uncle John Elder.

February 9, 1864

This evening, Tuesday, I arrived at the headquarters of General Humes. As I expected I found everybody in motion, himself on the field drilling. He drills the officers in person—makes them recite to him; is up late at night and early in the morning. I have "great expectation" of him. He met me very cordially and expressed gladness to have me with him once again. He is much changed in appearance since I met him. His wife is with him. I am to be something with him, I don't know what. I am to be self-sustaining in any place—recollect this—if I am to maintain independence and individuality—open to good examples and influences. All hope of going home is now dissipated and I can't tell when I will hear from my Belle.

February 10, 1864

This morning we left camp and moved 15 miles toward Rome. The Brigades moved ahead and I alone accompanied the General. I met Captain Scott and Lady at Oxford, Alabama and Cousin Will Crisp.

February 11, 1864
Headquarters, Humes Cavalry Brigade
Crop Plains

Today we have camped at Crop Plains, after traveling without incident fifteen miles. This evening after going into camp, General Kelly and staff rode up. I have been likened to General Kelly in personal appearance. I think it some compliment for, to youthful appearance is added quite a quick, intelligent look. His figure is fine—tall, straight and slight. He was appointed Brigadier General at the same time with General Humes, but owing to his having been Colonel before and Humes a Major, he over-ranks General Humes and is commanding Division. Well, tonight I have been assigned to duty on General Humes' staff as Acting Inspector General of this Brigade to report to the A.I.G. Well, what do I think of this? I am not satisfied—no, not by a great deal. I do not object to the rank, as I had no rank before, I , of course, cannot complain. No, on the other hand I am grateful. General Humes is very kind—yet he told me his A.I.G. was not an accomplished gentleman. At least not an educated man. Well, certainly I do not desire to be in subjection to an inferior kind of officer, and I do not think it complimentary for me to place me in subjection to such a man. It is true I have no experience in this kind of business, but my idea is that the duties are light and plain. Moreover, I think it is not what the General intended for me when he sent me the notice to report, because in his letter he says: "I think I can make you Inspector of my Brigade." In case of another of my friends being made Brigadier, he would have given me a higher place. But all other things being equal, I would rather be Lieutenant to General Humes than Captain to this other friend, who is still a

Colonel. I said I would accept any place the General might give me. Perhaps in this I was wrong. But patience! Perseverance and courage will make me <u>something.</u>

February 12, 1864
Tarapan Creek

This morning I was ordered out to inspect the disabled horses of this Brigade and send such as I thought unable to go on to the front, back to the rear. It was my first duty of this kind. The day was without incident.

February 13, 1864
Cave Springs

This evening I was ordered forward to inspect the camp and the brigade. The ground was bad and I found it difficult, yet I got it in order. Tonight I am in camp with headquarters at Cave Springs. I hear tonight that General Humes is to command Wharton's old Division, Wharton being ordered to the Transcript Department. I hope it is so.

February 18, 1864
Headquarters, First Cavalry Brigade, 4th Division
Near Rome, Georgia

My little journal, I have in some measure neglected you of late, though it has not been wanton neglect, but because of constant employment in other ways. We arrived here on the 14th, took up headquarters with a Mr. Mobly, who gives us all pleasant lodging and good eating. I am falling into the business ways of these headquarters and am in some measure wearing away the ennui and unrest which at first beset me. I find the staff officers thus far all pleasant and generally men of good business qualifications. Captain Walker, the A.A. General is refined and a business man, I think to a degree. He is in very feeble health. Lieutenant White is A.D.C. to the General. He is rather dashing, rather handsome, social enough and appears intelligent for his age. He is only 19 years old, from Huntsville, Alabama. The Q.M. is a large, fat, fine looking man, loves to eat, has a high reputation for being fun and is from Nashville. As yet the commissary has not arrived. All together we are a pleasant set of fellows and are having quite a pleasant time. The General is certainly one of the most energetic men I ever saw and more thoroughly inspects every department of business and labors more himself than any of his rank I have ever seen. He gives spirit and enterprise to all of his officers and men too who are much account. Many who have been in the habit of playing off, grumble a good deal, but all are catching the spirit of improvement which is working like leaven throughout the command. Bad news comes on the cold, wailing winds from Western and Central Mississippi. The impudent enemy seem stalking along without rebuke or disaster into the heart of Mississippi and almost into Alabama. Already Meridian, the center of River Road facility has fallen into their widespread grasp without show of resistance. Meridian, where only three weeks ago I thought to bring my wife because I considered it easy of access to me from almost anywhere in the Confederacy and as much a refuge from danger of invasion as anywhere. I am glad I did not bring my darling wife to be tossed on the wild billows of this stormy way and frightened by the cruel threats of our inhuman foe. Poor Elijah and Joe! I wonder where the flushed birds have flown—so soon driven from their exile home, where they promised themselves happy homes, though all alone from kindred and friends. Verily our relentless enemies will have many sins to answer for in the day of retribution. Wish I knew where the homeless wanderers had gone. I want to hear from them very much. But my heart sinks when I think of you, my darling Belle. The favored time, if it had been my own, alas, to see you has gone and spring and summer may unfold to us visions of war that will dim our vision and shade our hearts. Wide distances spread out beyond my sight. Mountains and enemies between us. Ah! cold and selfish and sinful are the hearts of almost all humanity. Belle, I have not heard from you in more than two months. The letters are now mouldering in Grenada I expect for me. War…Belle, may we soon meet. God grant we may meet in love and joy.

February 21, 1864

This morning we moved at 6 A.M. traveling on without incident or interest until we approached the mountains over which we had to pass. Now commenced a slow, winding ascent, rising gradually higher—the wind blowing, the ground frozen and the cold bleak rocks covered with ice. Occasionally a horse was thrown. "Orion" was barefooted and could scarcely walk, so I dismounted and led him, lost in wonder at the great, rugged work of nature. What fearful agonies must have convulsed the earth when these giant rocks and hills were torn from the bonds of this Mother Earth. Sometimes the road lay through solid rock, and way above, threatening and grim, hung the big rocks by a small tenure which looked as though they might break away from their base and come tumbling, crushing and grinding on columns of cavalry and everything impending, as if to show how old these mountains were and

how defiant of time. As we gained the summit, I almost
expected to see the mountain goats standing lovely and bold
on their jagged cliffs and then all would have reminded one of
the grand old ways which Walter Scott has so graphically and
poetically described. When we gained the summit, I looked
back and there winding in the distance was our cavalcade,
dragging its slow length still in the rear, looking like shadows
of wagons. Away still further in the valley shone the squatters
cabins that here and there dotted the plain, looking small as
the play houses I used to build in the gleeful days of little
boyhood. Like a giant serpent dragging its length along, our
column wound down the mountain towards Dalton—soon to
be the scene of another great, sad tragedy. In Dalton I went to
seek out my old chum, Grigsby Jack. I found he was at a
hospital set apart for smallpox, yet there were no cases there. I
determined to go anyhow. It was amusing to see me taking
[unkn] on the place and keeping on the windward side and
finally to have old Jack make his appearance, fat and more
Grigsbyish than ever in looks; to see me halt him until he said
there was no danger—then we met—we, who had once been
so frolic—yet that had not met in almost two years, again
clasped hands, again were smiling and talking in unison of
gleeful old times and places and dear old friends. Oh, me! we
spoke rather gloomily of our sad situation as to home and
loved ones. Neither of us had heard from home in a long time
and a long time [unkn] we would. How little we know the
future—its hidden joys and sorrows, for in a very short time
we walked over to our headquarters where each of us was
handed a letter. Oh, gladness! Joy beyond measure; gratitude
deep to God! A letter from my wife, my Belle! Oh, how like
magic did fade away the sadness which Grigsby said had

settled on me since he had seen me last. Well might I have been sad when the hopes I had cherished of soon seeing my loved Belle had all been crushed and I had found no one to whom I could speak her name scarcely. Many of General Humes' staff with whom I had been daily associated since I have been here do not suspect that I am married. How little they know of what I am, of my inner life, of the constant thoughts of my mind, of the deepest feeling of my heart. When I am silent they may think me [unkn]. When my soul is dwelling with thine, dearest, they may think me absent-minded. God keep you darling. It was a dear letter. Long, like you always write me; tender and sweet and loving as yourself. We got no news of local interest, but each word was of deeper interest to us than any other ones could be. My darling was well and <u>patient</u>. Oh, wife you are a marvel. She has sent me a new suit of clothing. I doubt if I get them, as they were sent by Genada. She is anxious to hear from me and thank Providence ere now, many and long letters have reached her, though not since I have been in this department. Darling, I hope to see you soon. Will I? God grant I may. Grigsby and I parted the next morning. I think he assumes an air of indifference about many things which he does not feel.

February 22, 1864

Ordered to the front—home after dark.

February 23, 1864

Federals advancing. Are here. Skirmishing has commenced. We fell back about two miles and camped for the night. Lost one man killed, a stranger who happened to fall into our ranks.

February 24, 1864

This morning skirmishing has again commenced—the enemy pressing us. They have maneuvered for a long time. Now they are displaying a large force of infantry. I have heard bullets that seemed very close. Our Sergeant of Comm. was shot—had his left broken [sic] was just behind the General and myself who were riding together. Several horses were shot. Captain Walker had his horse shot. The Yankee sharpshooters were on the mountains and they could distinguish the officers and they made good use of their opportunity. Cavalry is very unwieldy and very much disposed to make a coward of a good soldier. We are in comfortable headquarters—looking on the morrow for a great, sad conflict, as the Yankees have moved up and confronted our army.

February 25, 1864
Battlefield Headquarters

This morning we awoke early and all immediately prepared themselves, mostly in silence, for the great battle which we expected to bear a part in. Deep thought was manifest on each face. A determined air was worn by many. Some were pale, fidgety and nervous. Soon we could hear the sharp, quick report of the picket guns ringing out on the clear, still morning. Now the fire grows nearer. Now you hear the whistling of a bullet—now none, and already the deep, heavy guns are booming their solemn notes. Already our cavalry is sweeping around to the left to take position, and soon there is action—a scattering and rearing of horse; the enemy has discerned us and opened a battery on us. We gallop at the head of the column to let the rear get out of range. We move out and form in the open field for a charge. We remain for a while and then again we are discerned. Now again the battery opens. We hear the whining, whishing on of the ball. It falls just in front and does no harm. We know others are coming and we look to see the burst of smoke. It comes and falls in our column and frightens horses and men. Another comes and ranges just in our ranks. Still the dread boom is heard and the more dreaded monster shot speeds on and falls beside General Humes and staff, hitting the senior surgeon's horse. Another comes and hearts are beating high and eyes are wide aglow. Soon the excitement is rendered more intense, for a buzzing thing strikes the ground about one hundred yards in our front and ricochets and falls immediately in front of General Humes and staff, —not more than twenty feet from us. Now General Wheeler orders our cavalry to fall back where the enemy can't see us. We do so, not, however, before one or two more shells fall in the column. Still the skirmishing has continued, but not very heavily. But now the conflict deepens. The enemy come up and engage our line of infantry on the right of our army line and just on the left of our front. Now the lines are meeting, now the musketry bursts into one continuous, deafening, appalling roar, and cannon in the interval render the roar more like the tempest and thunder breaking on the Alpine Hills, as described by Scott. I can hear the cheers in the distance, and the boys' cry; there is the Rebel halloo, and sure enough backward are pushed the Federal battle lines. This heavy fire lasts only about half an hour, and it ceases. Only two of our Brigades now engaged. Night, the conflict of the day is succeeded by a calm as deep and still as if our camp fires and the enemies blazed not in the view of each. We are in our headquarters of last night. Here, too, is the vestige of war.

A house burned, the furniture all removed. Remnants lie scattered around. We are preserved, thank God!

February 26, 1864

This morning we were ordered to our positions of yesterday. Last night we all thought that the dawn of today would usher in one of the greatest conflicts of the war. We looked eagerly on each other last night, as we sat around the fire, for we felt that we might not all sit together again. As light was breaking over the hills where still in line lay our brave hero rebels, we sprung up and in silence prepared for the day and the struggle. We watched anxiously for the opening of the great tragedy. Deep anxiety sat on each face—deep feeling was in every heart. Minutes and even hours passed on and speculation was heard on every side. Some said the storm would soon burst. "They maneuver," says one. "It is an ominous calm, " says another. "Soon we will have it in earnest." But time passed and still no attack. Speculation again was at work. But soon we had the solution. They were rapidly falling back and had been since 10 or 11 o'clock last night. Then our cavalry advanced at a gallop to find them. Now they were encamped, here they had a battery, here they left a bed; here they killed fowls, here was a pool of blood, here a dead horse, and here a Yankee. On we go for five miles, when "whiz" goes a bullet and we all say "Here are the Yankees." Now we skirmish fight for several miles. They killed one brave soldier and one horse. One of the Colonels had his horse shot dead; another a thumb shot off. We penetrated about eight miles from Dalton, then returned behind our infantry. Cavalry and (unkn) took up quarters in our old headquarters where we had lodged safely through Providential goodness for three nights.

February 27, 1864

Last night my horse got loose and some mean person stole my halter and part of my bridle, so this morning I had to go to Ordinance Headquarters to try to get a bridle. While gone the Brigade moved on the Ringgold Road. The enemy last night moved back from in front of our center. I was not with the Brigade today, but they skirmished some—without injury, however.

February 28, 1864

We have established headquarters in the town of Tunnel Hill. Have a nice headquarters. Today walked through the tunnel.

February 29, 1864

Last night I was sent to the front to inspect pickets. Enemy in Ringgold, about four miles from us. All quiet on the front.

March 2, 1864
Headquarters, Tunnel Hill

Yesterday evening it was announced that a flag of truce was in our front, on the Ringgold Road at our Vedette pickets. We commenced to make preparations for meeting it. The ostensible purpose of the flag was the exchanging of three wounded soldiers which they were due us by previous conditions of exchange. The Yankees are very shrewd, though, and very frequently kill two birds with one stone, and I thought by the tenor of their questions that they probably had ulterior designs. Few of them said anything to me though of what was uppermost in our minds—the political condition of the country. They were all very fine looking, fine appearing men. They were very courteous and sociable—very generous and rather prodigal. They reminded me of the time when before the war college boys would meet, and in the profusion of money and whiskey each would vie with the other in wild expenditure. We Rebels had to act the poor boys for we had no intimation before of our going. I was told by General Humes to saddle my horse and I supposed I was to visit the outposts, but I was ordered to go with Colonel Prather who commanded on our side. We carried a few papers with us, such as we could find in our office. They brought us many papers and magazines and they had a profusion of whiskey and drank it very freely. Several of them were improperly light. They sent presents to several of our officers and spoke in gallant style of many of them. I saw no disposition among them to evince a superiority to our men in anything. Many, indeed all of them, expressed a great desire for this cruel war to close, when we could meet in friendly circles, in social familiarity, under one flag, and be one again. It will not be. Such meetings live only in song or story or history. Such meetings will be eventful in the future. Colonel Burke, 10th Ohio Infantry, commanded. Lieutenant Colonel Ward, 10th Ohio Infantry was along. C.C. Cramsony of the same Regiment and headquarters guide to General Thomas was of the party. He was very gallant to me; took my card and told me to call on him if I found myself in his army. Wonder if he would do anything for me? John Van Demur, 35th Ohio Infantry Regiment was along. He was Regt. Quartermaster. He was very sociable and generous for he told me he would be pleased to meet me in the future in peace and in addition gave me a shin plaster 5 cents and in return I gave him fifty cents and I also gave Lt. Reynolds a fifty cent shin plaster. Lieut. Reynolds was AAAG to General Thomas' staff. Was very pleasant little fellow. There were two majors along whose names I have forgotten. I had a long talk with one of them. He said any man who would insult our friends behind the lines, mistreat soldiers when prisoners or abuse or malign the great foe they were contending against was a coward and had never visited the front. We returned with expressions of well wishes on both sides.

March 4, 1864

Today I have visited the Tennessee troops, where long ago I used to serve—the old 4th Regiment Infantry—the men with whom I had stood up on one of the saddest and bloodiest days I have ever looked on and lived through. Shiloh!—full of such scenes and sudden memories. I have not seen this old 4th Regiment since a few days after that day. All—even my enemies—met me with gladness and crowded around me as though anxious to see how I looked. And my friends were eager and enthusiastic in their greetings. One said— "He is Charley still"—Another—"How I wish you were with us still—all miss you." "How I want to go with you, etc." Many of my friends and acquaintances are now in the 47th Tennessee Regiment and these I did not see at all. Was very unwell today. I could scarcely tear myself away from them. Another day I will go and see them. Many sad chances have passed over them since I saw them before. I asked myself where were some faces plain to view in memory—yet a dead silence hung, choking and stifling away the answers. And I know these faces have decayed. I know those forms sleep in shallow graves on the strange, tragic hillsides of Perryville and Murfreesboro. Out of those who had been almost one hundred when we left Trenton on the 15th of May, 1861— with jest and drink and cheer and toast in the fog of the dawning morning—in hearing of scoffs and compliments—in hearing of sobs and farewells—in sight of waving hands and banners. Many hearts, young and bold, which then fluttered with pride and pleasure and honor, have since known the darkest sorrow which ever, ever gloomed and palled the being of any people. Of all that band of strong men, in but thirteen hearts of that old West Tennessee Rifles now flows and ebbs the flood tide of life.

March 8, 1864

Yesterday I was called upon to witness one of the saddest scenes I have almost ever seen. The execution of one of our soldiers by hanging. One man executed by the laws of war. A brave soldier brought to ignominious death on the gibbet of desertion—desertion to the enemy. He was the first man I have ever seen executed in any way. The scene was one of awing solemnity to me. The idea of the great loss our country has in this war sustained—the idea of a man one moment in the possession of life and health, in this condition sitting on the coffin in a few moments to hold his lifeless body, looking on the scaffold which is to consign him to a convict's grave looking on a large assemblage of curious persons, knowing that in all this great concourse not one was perhaps breathing a prayer for his spirit's rest or murmuring a word of sympathy for him in this great and sad time. He sees the flag of his country—the banner of his army, 'neath the folds of which he has marched in the midst of death and victory. He knows that a word could prolong his miserable life, that a word might save him. He sees no relent. He knows from the cold, firm look that there can be no hope for him. He sees the executioner, the rope is coiled cold and strong around his neck, soon to be broken. Chains are clanking on his feet, soon to be dangling in the air. His eyes look calmly on the great crowd. His lips murmur, I suppose I prayer. He knows death, dishonorable death is just before him. His old companions in the spots of boyhood, his associates as men, his comrades in arms are all around him. For what? to see him die—to see him die on the gallows. As the time draws near for his execution he murmurs a prayer aloud. Oh, I wish he could live!

March 9, 1864
Headquarters

Joyous news, little Journal. Last night I wrote a letter to my Belle. Last night. Rather a glad letter. I think and hope my Belle will find it decidedly so. This morning I forwarded it direct to her. May it reach her and speedily. Today I sat in my room, and I was thinking of home, thinking deeply of home and as usual I was rather sad in my thoughts. Now and then someone would come in the room. I would look up listlessly and then think on. I wanted to go home. I couldn't. I wanted to hear from home. I couldn't. I wanted to send home and I couldn't. My Belle, my heart is longing for you. Oh, Belle, when will this separation be no more? After a time someone came in with the mail. I did not look up for I thought I had no correspondents south of the lines. One of the clerks looked up and called "Charley" and halted. I looked up and coldly smiled. I thought he was trying to tease me. Yet he handed me a letter in a strange hand and postmarked "Atlanta." It was heavy—in this respect it was like Belle's. Hastily I broke the seal—somewhat nervously. Joy! Smiles! It is a letter forwarded from Belle. Dearest wife. You are still patient, waiting, longing, praying. Thank God, you are well—all well at home. Dear loved one, my heart is waiting too. Oh, may it not be long that our hearts must wait.

March 20, 1864
Headquarters

Little Journal I make the most pleasing record in you it has ever been my fortune to make since our pleasant yet brief acquaintance. It is this. I have a <u>furlough</u>. Ah, yes! I have a furlough to go home. Glad is my heart tonight. Though my furlough is short and it will afford me little time to stay at home—yet it will be home. Home, to see it! To look on it! To delight in it, even though for an hour! I feel like I would go if only for six hours to see my Belle. Ah, what will she say— what do—how look? Will I surprise her? Will I find laughing and joy? Oh, home. My mother is there, my friends, a charming circle of beautiful and joyous loved ones. Sisters and brothers. My dear father. You, too, will welcome your buffetted soldier boy. My wife will we meet soon? It is a long, rough way, a dangerous, toilsome way; yet I am going to brave time and toil and danger and my own, I would brave a thousandfold for you. This day—this holy Sabbath day one week ago, while sad, while thinking of you, a letter came from you to me, full of love and patience. My wife, you are worthy of one greater and better than your Charley.

March 21, 1864
Headquarters, Laurel Hill

Well, companion of my way-faring life, Well! Now! This record is made with an agitated feeling. My hand is tremulous and so is my heart. I am glad and yet a feeling of fear lies, stirs under it all. I am about to set out on a perilous journey. If I am spared to accomplish it a rapture of bliss is awaiting me. If I am overtaken by the Federals a painful, maybe a long captivity awaits me away from loved ones—even from sympathy. If my Belle only knew tonight what is before me, her heart would leap and smile in alternate joy and fear and how earnestly would she pray God for my speedy and safe coming. She has or will pray God for me this night and maybe her heart in silent communion with mine, has caught the impression of my coming. Yes, God, our Heavenly Father, can bring me safely to you and on Him I trust—to Him I pray. God grant me speedy and safe passage to the gentle heart and arms of my waiting, patient Belle, with the pleasing assurance that all will be well. I go early tomorrow and am hoping and trusting to be at home Friday week. Tomorrow is Tuesday.

March 22, 1864
Headquarters

Ah, what a morning, what a distressing morning! Frowning so heavily—so white is all the earth—yet I am going to start home. God speed me.

March 22, 1864
At Mr. Kendricks. Night

I have traveled today through and over snow about 37 miles. Have had no difficulty thus far. May this auger me safely in all the trip.

March 23, 1864

Tonight we are stopping at Mr. Hale's. Common fare. Today we have traveled 37 miles. I am so weary of this slow motion. Today we passed some falls—water falling thirty or forty feet. We are within 16 miles of Gadsden. Mr. King, a young man from Memphis, is traveling with me. We are thus far mercifully preserved. Be it so even to the end.

Waterfall near Gadsden, Alabama,
mentioned by Charles on March 23, 1864.
Photograph courtesy of Kirk Hays Lane.

March 24, 1864

This evening we find ourselves at Mr. Campbell's, 25 miles from Gadsden. Last night we stayed 16 miles the other side of Gadsden, making our travel yesterday 41 miles. Today we passed over some ground once the scene of a skirmish between our great Forrest and the notorious Straight. Saw where several cannon shot had struck the trees. We are traveling now the road Straight traveled on his home raid. Tonight we have overtaken a party of Tennesseans destined for our route for a day's travel or so and we will probably travel together for a time. We may be of mutual support to each other. Thus far we are preserved. We met tonight also a party of gentlemen from middle Tennessee who gave us some valuable information about the Mother country. Oh, for safety to the end!

March 25, 1864
Friday

As days pass, dear Belle, I near you slowly. Mountains and rivers are behind me. Tonight we have first rumors of the enemy ahead, almost immediately in our front. Tomorrow if I am spared I will be out of great danger. Direct and preserve me. Oh, Father! Tonight we are stopping with a Mr. Simms. Today we have traveled 38 miles. This country here is almost altogether Union and barren as a desert. It is with very great difficulty we can procure anything either for ourselves or horses. "Orion" is much worn. Today or rather last night I met with a clubmate of mine. T.H.O. Lieutenant Wilson.

March 26, 1864
Saturday

Today we have traveled hard and far, over a country infested by the very demon of war. Bushwhackers, Yankees, Union citizens! Mountains jagged with sharp rocks, steep hills and deep grades. All were inimical to our pleasant travel. Yet tonight I am at Mr. Ervins, four miles from Moulton North Road. We have been mercifully preserved, and now are out of danger. Traveled 38 miles.

March 27, 1864
Sunday Night

Tonight we stopped at a Mr. Greenhill 5 miles west of Frankfort. Today we have ridden through a country said to be infested slightly with Tories. We have not encountered any. Had no difficulty and met with a kind hospitable gentleman to entertain us for the night. Today has been a beautiful, balmy spring day. It has been a day for me of much thought—calm and silent. Thus far we have met little difficulty enroute. So may it be to the dear end. Traveled 36 miles.

March 28, 1864
Monday Night

This morning we found the rain falling, the clouds heavy. Yet we started off and finally the day cleared up; the wind rose and we augured for ourselves a pleasant day. Yet we were destined to be deluded, for late this evening, almost two hours before night, the clouds gathered, the thunder was heavy, and soon the heaviest rain I almost ever saw fell—wetting me through my overcoat, boots and small clothes almost immediately. We soon came to Iuka and here how very sad the view which met our gaze. The town wrecked entirely—save a few dwellings—doors, floors, and windows all gone and not a building in which was any business. We immediately started out of town for Burnside; rode rapidly and yet night came on us, and in Burnside no entertainment could be had either for horses or men. How vexing—how trying—how mean! Wet, weary, and hungry and yet no place to rest. Finally though, a family did receive us when we could go nowhere else. I am now in a nice parlor, my "Orion" stabled and fed. Thy power has kept us Oh, Father, and with Thy help tomorrow night we will reach Tennessee. Today we have traveled 43 miles.

March 29, 1864
Tuesday

Today we have traveled over a country for many miles entirely desolated. We have traveled today through a country over which the Federal General Halleck made his celebrated advance on Corinth after the battle of Shiloh. He fortified as he advanced and today we passed four different lines of fortifications on the road of his advance. They seemed to me though, to be very inadequate for the defense of a great army in case of attack being made on it. This portion of country and all around Iuka and Corinth is a waste and desolation. It made me very sad to travel through it. Everything and everybody looks ruined and really they are so. Even the women, once so fair and so elegant in appearance, now seem to a great extent shorn of both. It is a marvel how they subsist at all. War! War! How tragically awful—how sadly fearful thou art. Yet man— ah, most live on and think not of those who suffer. The heart has lost charity, sympathy and goodwill and people seem recklessly striding, plunging on—caring and providing for present life. Self is their idol!

Today "my name is MacGregor and my foot is on my native heath."[1] Land of pride, state of my love, clime of my birth! Today my longing gaze rested with gladness on thy fair shores. Tonight I am staying with Mr. Hendricks, a patriot Tennessean, two miles from Purdy. Two nights, my Belle, and with the help of our Father who has guided and kept me thus on my way of peril and you will rest in your Charley's arms on your Charley's heart. Today I traveled 35 miles. Tomorrow Mr. King leaves me and my way will be alone. Yet in thought I will have company.

March 30, 1864
Wednesday Night

Tonight I am stopping three miles north of Jackson, Tennessee. Once more I am here, loyal, glorious loved Tennessee. Once more amid the style and luxury and refinement of my homeland. Once more I am nearing the home where repose in kindness and peace all who are dearest to me on earth. They are ignorant of my coming. They are perhaps wishing for me. They talk of me and say "Oh, that Charley were here tonight." They little dream that their truant rebel is near them and tomorrow might will be with them. Belle, you darling, do you know that your boy is within 25 miles of your smiles and arms? Oh, Father thou who has thus far preserved me, grant me joy in going home. Today I have traveled 35 miles. Tonight "Orion" would scarcely move. Poor horse—so weary.

---

[1] From Sir Walter Scott's *Rob Roy*.

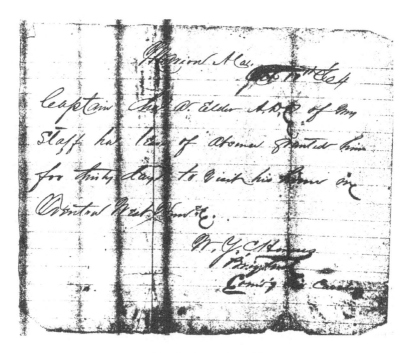

(Charley's Furlough)

Marion, Ala.

Oct. 17th '64

Captain Chas. A. Elder, A.D.C. of my
staff has leave of absence granted him
for thirty days to visit his home
in Central West Tennessee.

W.Y.C. Humes
Brig. Gen'l.
Comm'd'g ?? Cavalry

Note

But furloughs are short and wars are long. And every man was sorely needed in those last, dark days of the Confederacy.

Captain Elder and "Orion" were soon back with Wheeler and Humes and their courageous cavalrymen riding always between the advancing men in blue and the retreating and diminishing forces in gray.

Official reports show that during this last year of the war, Wheeler's cavalry with Humes as a brigade commander, and Elder was Humes' acting adjutant and aide de camp started this last campaign with around 4,000 men, and although during the year, he lost 3,200 men and officers, he recruited enough new men to keep his strength up to 3,887 at the time of his last report on April 20, 1865 (a few days after General Lee had surrendered). This Confederate Cavalry force maintained such a grueling pace and such constant conflict with the enemy that Wheeler had to replace nearly 100% casualties during this fateful year from the winter of 1864 to the spring of 1865.

But official reports also show that during this final year of battle, Wheeler had captured (not to mention other casualties inflicted) more than 7,000 of the enemy, together with 600 wagons, 2,000 mules, and 4,000 cavalry horses. Wheeler was in constant action, protecting the rear of the Confederate forces in east Alabama, Georgia, and South Carolina as they continually fell back from a larger enemy army. Wheeler, fighting a continuous rear guard action, averaged a daily movement with his cavalry crops of twenty miles. During this time, he had crossed thirty rivers with his forces and, on one raid into enemy territory, had spent two months behind enemy lines. One Federal correspondent wrote: *"The rebel cavalry under Wheeler fought our advances with an abandon and desperation worthy of a better cause."*

The gloom of these difficult days toward the end of the war is reflected in a brief report written by Captain Elder, as Humes' aide de camp and acting adjutant, to the acting adjutant of General Wheeler's headquarters, which recited the seriousness of the situation confronting Humes' Brigade at that time. In this letter which is now a part of official records in Washington, Captain Elder wrote:

HEADQUARTERS HUMES' DIVISION CAVALRY
February 2, 1865

Lieutenant Hudson,
Acting Assistant Adjutant-General, Wheeler's Corp:
Lieutenant: The enemy are now in one mile of our headquarters. General Humes moved early this morning to the Salkehatchie Road to meet the enemy. He left only one regiment (Fifth Tennessee) here. We cannot stop the enemy long. General Humes ordered the bridges destroyed across Salkehatchie Swamp. This will be done if possible. The enemy are pressing very hard. I sent General Humes a courier informing him that he could not return by way of his old headquarters. His wagon trains are moving toward Duck Branch Post Office. I thought proper to inform you of this.
Very respectfully, Lieutenant, your obedient servant,
CHAS. A ELDER
Aide-de-Camp

Then Humes, in these wearisome days of late winter and early spring of 1865, was leading his brigade of Wheeler's cavalry in constant combat around the Selkehatchie River, Whippy

Swamp, Buford's Bridge, and other places in South Carolina as they protected the Confederate Army in its withdrawal toward Columbia and Augusta. In leading a charge of his brigade on March 10, 1865, General Humes was severely wounded. So, the war entered a new and ending phase for Captain Elder, who stayed with his General and went with him to the field hospitals.

Belle's Diary

And as the war gradually progressed to its bitter end, Belle Bright never ceased confiding in her "little book." Somewhere near the end of the war, although Captain Elder, her Charley had not yet returned home as a free man, Belle entered in her diary:

March 15, 1865

I have $25-Tenn in my purse. I design buying a pair of cavalry boots for Charley, which will require, I think, $24.

April 8, 1865

Four months today since Charley left me and I sit here tonight a changed being in some respects, but not as yet happy, not as yet "anchored" in a "Sweet Content". Strange I should not write that to him, my dearest friend. No, to none, little book but to you. I dislike melancholy. It is vain and selfish. I believe for a long time, five or six or seven years, indeed nearly all my life, I've known little of joy, a free careless spirit, and yet I hardly think my nature is prone to melancholy, save as circumstances have made it. It is very, very seldom my heart is free from a care.

Note

And then the war is over, and Belle Bright and Charles Elder, for the first time in so long a while look for a permanent furlough from the sadness and separation of war. Captain Elder, at Columbus, Kentucky, where he had trained with his first Regiment, the 4th Tennessee Volunteers, and where they had seen their first shots "fired in anger" as they skirmished with the enemy across the river in Missouri in those early days when the South sought to tie Missouri and Kentucky to its side, was paroled by a Federal officer. On May 21, 1865, Captain Elder pledges never again to bear arms against the United States of America.

And then, with new hopes and new vision, as Charley comes home to assume his task of re-establishing his fortunes so that he may provide for his family, Belle Bright writes:

October 17, 1865

Little book, look upon me, I am a changed woman from what I was when I wrote in you last. Little friend, I've had a very sweet mercy lately, I've been to visit my husband in St. Louis. Oh, how happy…how blessed! I am back again, back at my old duties. Do you know, I have a very sweet hope before me…a hope e're very long to join my husband and to remain with him. Well, I have had this desire a very long time, this desire that grew to be a yearning, a yearning that had so much of aching with it…for, ah, it seemed so dim…so unpromising, save in God's mercy. This desire, yearned for, for four years, four years of heart straining, heart trial. God alone knows how great, and now I see it ahead of me.

(Charley's oath of allegiance to the United States of America)

I Charles A. Elder, Capt. and A.D.C. on Brig Gen'l Humes Staff C.S.A. do hereby give my solemn parole of honor not to bear arms against the United States of America nor aid or assist any of her enemies whatsoever or until properly exchanged by the authorized Commissioner of exchange.

Chas. A. Elder
Capt. A.D.C.

Sworn and subscribed before me this 21st day of May 1865

W.S. Lansing
Major 4th U.S.A. Calvary

November 5, 1865

Seven more weeks, little bonny book, seven more weeks, and what? Now, listen, remember the war, remember now, re-enter your old existence, feel its longing, pray its prayers, hope its hopes, wait, yearn, have your spirit strained to its old tension, have a sweet season and sicken again at its transientness, have it to pass and the old life so hard renewed...these! Have you done this, well, then you are ready to know what lieth at the end of seven weeks. Life with my husband, Peace! Ah, little bonny book, I'm just now in radiance of one of the soft moonbeams of hope, life. So long dark, very dark, little book. You and I know how hard and dark. It is now becoming silvered. Its horizon seems lightened some, oh, may it, may it, may it come, glad soul these are rejoicing days!

Note

But for Charles Elder, an old, young man of twenty-seven and his old, young wife of twenty-three there were two more years of economic struggle, trial, separation, and tribulation before Belle Bright Elder writes:

September 8, 1867

Sabbath. Since I wrote in you last, little book, how many changes have passed into our lives. Oh, may I be thankful to God for his continued mercies! Oh, may His blessing be upon us through life. Tonight, a beautiful moonlit night, calm, pleasant. I sit in the unfinished parlor of Eldersley, five miles from Trenton. My girl baby, seven months old, sleeps on the bed. My husband, absent from me in Cincinnati, where he has been on business.

Little quiet, gentle, book, I look for my dear husband tomorrow. You and I have talked about his coming. Let us have a long talk about it this morning. You shall advise me what I must do in every particular to make him happy…to be worthy of his love.

End

Belle (this page) and Charley (facing page) in later years.
Photographs courtesy of Kirk Hays Lane.

Tombstone of Belle and Charles Elder,
Oakland Cemetery, Trenton, Tennessee.
Photograph courtesy of Kirk Hays Lane.

Acknowledgments

These journals and the narrative research are dedicated to my late Uncle Robert Dudley Hays, for his exhaustive efforts to try to get them published. Charley and Belle Elder were his grandparents. Many thanks to his daughter, Ann Tiffin Hays Cowden, for preserving and cherishing these diaries. Thanks also to Charley and Belle's great-granddaughters, Kirk Hays Lane and Bright Hays for much historical information and fill-ins. Also thanks to my wife, Ilse Hays, for her research and encouragement as well as her tireless efforts in getting these works published.

Charley Elder survived that awful war, and he and Belle went on to raise seven children. Their fourth daughter was my great-grandmother, Bonny. She was, by all accounts, an absolutely elegant lady who lamented all her life the destruction wrought upon the South by the Yankees, yet when visitors from the North would come to call, she would always receive them with graciousness and hospitality; always a lady.

Charley died in 1899, Belle in 1920. Both are buried in Oakland Cemetery in Trenton, Tennessee.

Andrew Hays
Winchester, Virginia

Made in the USA
Middletown, DE
30 April 2022

65044508R00046